June 2016,
Fernando Stock Newsletter,

Lalana Fernando

CONTENTS

1 SCORCARD

Name	Initial Purchase Dt	Average Cost per share in $	Number of shares purchased (or multiples of it)	Total Cost of our purchase in $	5/31/16 share price in $	Current Market Value in $	Total Gain or (Loss) in $	Total Gain or (Loss) as a %
Glaxo Smith Kline	11/2/15	41.36	15	620.40	42.74	641.10	20.70	3.34%
Twitter	8/3/15	25.14	20	502.80	15.49	309.80	(193.00)	-38.39%
General Motors	8/24/15	24.62	10	246.20	31.62	316.20	70.00	28.43%
Ford	8/24/15	10.44	10	104.40	13.56	135.60	31.20	29.89%
General Electric	8/24/15	19.37	10	193.70	30.34	303.40	109.70	56.63%
Exxon Mobil	8/24/15	66.55	4	266.20	90.20	360.80	94.60	35.54%
Chevron	1/10/16	79.77	2	159.54	102.28	204.56	45.02	28.22%
IBM	1/25/16	121.64	2	243.28	153.81	307.62	64.34	26.45%
Schlumberger Limited (SLB)-	1/25/16	63.23	2	126.46	77.60	155.20	28.74	22.73%
Valley National Bancorp	1/19/16	8.59	5	42.95	9.61	48.05	5.10	11.87%
Canadian Index EWC	1/19/16	18.68	3	56.04	24.82	74.46	18.42	32.87%
Bank of America	1/10/16	13.67	5	68.35	15.05	75.25	6.90	10.10%
Disney	1/10/16	94.47	2	188.94	99.89	199.78	10.84	5.74%
Alcoa	8/24/15	7.97	10	79.70	9.48	94.80	15.10	18.95%
Apple	8/24/15	93.01	19	1,767.19	100.40	1,907.60	140.41	7.95%
TOTAL, as of 5/31/16				4,666.15		5,134.22	468.07	10.03%
Gain (or Loss) For May.2016				909.36		5,134.22	159.01	17.49%

Month and Year	Total Cost of our purchase in $	Current Market Value in $	Total Gain or (Loss) in $	Total Gain or (Loss) as a %
Gain (or Loss) For May.2016	909.36	5,134.22	159.01	**17.49%**
Gain (or Loss) For April.2016		4,065.85	(74.12)	**-1.79%**
Gain (or Loss) For Mar.2016		4,139.97	383.22	**9.59%**
Gain (or Loss) For Feb.2016	396.47	3,995.79	(266.06)	**-6.88%**
Gain (or Loss) For Jan.2016	899.97	3,865.38	283.07	**10.55%**
Gain (or Loss) For Dec.2015		2,682.34	(169.47)	-6.10%
Gain (or Loss) For Nov.2015		2,777.29	480.81	**20.94%**
Gain(or Loss) For October 2015		2,296.48	231.40	**11.21%**
Gain(or Loss) For September 2015		2,065.08	(2.26)	-0.11%
Gain(or Loss) as of 9/1/15 (or Aug. 2015)		2,067.34	316.74	**18.09%**

2 WHAT IS NEW SINCE LAST EDITION

As you can see from our scorecard, our portfolio rose by 17.49% between 4/30/16 and 5/31/16 !! During the same period, the stock market or the S&P500 index (top 500 companies) rose only by 1.5%. Even our worst pick Twitter rose by 5.95% between 5/1/16 and 5/31/16. In order to have a general idea where we are headed for the market, we have to consider what the technical analysts (chartists who are in to Fibonacci ratios etc.) say and when most of them agree, then it is very credible. For the past 18 months, the market has been range bound. If the market has been range bound for more than a year, and it breaks it to the upside we could have a big gain (i.e. even 20%). Also if the market does not have a break through to the upside, once again we could have another severe correction. Chartists say that small cap stocks (Russell 2000) is indicating that it is ready to move much higher. However, many money managers are selling their stocks and waiting for the market to make new highs to get back in to the market. I personally think that is a stupid idea. We can buy more as the market moves lower and reduce the average cost. So what is the magic level all these technicians are watching for? It is around 2134 on the S&P500; the S&P500 has to go over 2134 and stay there for a while or else it would be risky to assume that the market is going to go much higher. May 2016 is different from May 2015 as the market is technically stronger. As of now, 75% of the stocks are above their 200 day moving average. When a stock goes below its 200 day moving average, it is in dangerous territory and most prudent investors would stay away from those stocks. International markets and economies are in better shape now than in May 2015. Oil reaching $50 per barrel in May 2016, is too a very good sign. On the negative side, per Barron's, Carl Icahn, one of the best activist investors, had a net short position of 149% at the end of first quarter 2016; at the end of 2015, his short position was net 25% and a year ago it was only 4%. So Icahn is betting the farm on a big correction or a crash!

Schlumberger- According to Bloomberg News, on 5/24/16, Goldman Sachs after being bearish on oil for years, added Schlumberger to its conviction buy list. Analyst Waqar Syed reiterated a $94 price target- nearly 30% above the stock price of 5/24/16.

Twitter- On 5/18/16, Ronnie Moas, issued a buy recommendation on Twitter as their cash position is at $3.6B and their market cap was at $10B with a PE of 23. Then on

5/10/16, Bob Peck of Suntrust, stated that the lowest we could see for Twitter should be $12 per share. He also stated that it is a candidate for getting acquired by another and Google is a possible suitor. He expects the price of Twitter to go up during the second half of 2016.

GM and Ford- As analysts have been expecting it was announced that auto sales have peaked. Car sales for some automakers were down as much as 30%. Due to low oil prices, most of the demand is for SUVs and trucks-globally. Hedge funds are getting out of GM. On 5/11/16, GM announced that it has finally turned a corner in Europe. Even though we cannot expect growth from these automakers, the auto market is expected to remain stable and profitable for a long time to come. GM is a PE of 5 and a yield around 5%, the stock is a safe place to park your money.

Apple- Right now this has the biggest risk and the biggest reward. "No risk, no reward". Day by day, the nay sayers are growing. More and more, pundits are saying that Apple will take the same road as Nokia, Xerox and Eastman Kodak (or even IBM). Latest is that Apple will take 3 years and not 2 to come up with a major change in the IPhone. Shark Tank's billionaire Kevin O'Leary who used to be a big fan of Apple for years and who also started his own ETFs known as O'Shares states that his new Samsung can do everything but wash his laundry and it will take ages for Apple to come to that stage. The most bearish people on Apple expect the share price to hit $85 by the latter part of 2016. To me, that is not bad at all. It hit $89 in May 2016. If it goes to $85, I suggest you buy 5 more shares and another 5 shares at $75. Carl Icahn got in to Apple years ago when it was a dud and he got Apple to be more shareholder friendly. During the past few weeks, he sold all his Apple holdings with a net profit of $4 Billion! Carl was worried that Apple might have more problems in China. In fact, one year ago, Carl said that he will never sell Apple. Then should everyone get out of Apple too? No, not by a long shot. I still have faith in Apple and more than that the greatest investor this world has ever known and the 2nd most richest man on Earth, Warren Buffet just bought $1 billion in Apple shares! For many decades, he avoided technology stocks till he got in to IBM which has been a dud for the longest time. IBM too is showing signs of turning around. On 5/12/16, Apple dropped below $90 for the first time in 2 years giving us another chance to increase our stake in Apple; also after a long time they dropped below Google aka Alphabet in market cap to $496B. On 5/13/16, Apple announced that they were going to invest $1B in China. Their profit margin is at 23% while the profit margin for their competitors is around 7% which could lead to a bigger problem for Apple. Apple makes a big deal about going in to India for the first time and how India is going to take over China as the most populated country; however keep in mind that per capita income of India (GDP/# of people) is US $1,500 per year and the monthly average wage in India is US $295. I cannot see a mad rush to buy a $700 IPhones. People will kill each other to steal an IPhone! On 5/2/16, Tim Cook, CEO of Apple, on CNBC show Mad Money stated the following:

- In China, other smart phone users turning to Apple is huge.
- In 2 years, Apple grew 70% in China.
- The middle class in China is growing from 50 million to 500 million in 5 years.
- India will be the most populous country in 2020 and most young people in India wants to own a smart phone.

3 PROFILE & BACKGROUND OF EACH STOCK

GlaxoSmithKline plc (GSK)

Current Price: $42.74

Initial Purchase: 11/2/15, buy 5 shares at $43.06 (or at lowest price on 11/2/15)

Current recommendation: buy 10 shares if share price drops below $37

Average cost with this purchase: $41.36

 Gain of 3.34% in 211 days (see scoreboard for calculations)

From last month:

As of 1/9/16, the dividend rate is at 5.91% and this is a solid company with a PE of 6.77-compare that with the industry average of 26! If the price drops to $37, then the dividend rate or yield will go up to 6.3%. If the price drops to $30, the yield will go up to 7.77%. This alone will attract investors in the future. The only concern is that the government might come up with price controls for this industry and that is a valid risk.

Recently Barron's had a very favorable article on Glaxo Smith Kline (GSK) and my own research shows that Barron's is on the right path. I do not always agree with Barron's. As of 11/1/15, the dividend rate is 6.98%!! That is 350% of the 10 year US Treasury rate! This is a company with a market cap of $104 Billion. With their recent acquisition of Novartis and with vaccines business and possible AIDS drugs, Barron's expect a 25% increase in price over the next 12 months. Don't count on that! Currently it is trading at $43 and if the price drops by 50% with no significant news, that is a 14% dividend yield from a solid pharma company based in UK. The dividend yield will act as a hedge against a major drop in the price of the stock. However this works only with companies that will not cut their dividends. This is a historic fact.

Twitter, Inc. (TWTR)

Current Price: $15.49

Initial Purchase: 8/3/15, buy 10 shares at $29.27

2nd Purchase: 8/24/15, buy 10 shares at $21.01

Current recommendation: Hold till price drops below $10 and buy 50 shares

Average cost with this purchase: $25.14 per share

Loss: 38.39% in 302 days

On 5/18/16, Ronnie Moas, issued a buy recommendation on Twitter as their cash position is at $3.6B and their market cap was at $10B with a PE of 23. Then on 5/10/16, Bob Peck of Suntrust, stated that the lowest we could see for Twitter should be $12 per share. He also stated that it is a candidate for getting acquired by another and Google is a possible suitor. He expects the price of Twitter to go up during the second half of 2016.

From last month:

For the past 3 months I have been wondering if we should sell Twitter as it is bringing down the whole portfolio down but for now, I intend to stick with Twitter. On of its greatest fans, Steve Bahlmer, former CEO of Microsoft tweeted on 3/10/16 that he sold his holdings of Twitter saying, "Twitter taught him not to be an investor". As I have said before, if the share price drops below $10, we should consider buying another 100 shares so as to bring down the average cost to $12.52 (50% reduction.

I initially recommended Twitter when everyone hated it. Then last month I stated that there was a rumor on Wall Street that the board was going to make Jack Dorsey the permanent CEO of Twitter; the very next day that happened and the stock went up by 6% in one day. There is a rumor that Google, Apple or Facebook might buy Twitter. Then what happened on 10/7/15, Saudi Prince Alaweed doubled his stake at Twitter to 5% and now he is the #2 owner of Twitter and he owns more shares than the founder and CEO, Jack Dorsey! This Saudi Prince is well respected on Wall Street and he is known to pick 'stock bottoms'. He still owns a major share of Citibank, 21st Century Fox etc. Then on 10/12/15, Twitter announced that they were cutting their global labor force by 8% and they have the lowest pay rates compared to their competitors. On the same day, Jim Cramer predicted that the price of Twitter would go up. The good news on Twitter kept on flowing like a tidal wave in October 2015! On 10/16/15, former CEO of Microsoft, Steve Ballmer, sent a tweet, "Good job, Twitter! I am glad that I just bought 4% of your company". Now Ballmer and Alaweed owns more of Twitter than CEO Dorsey! Then a few days ago, CEO Dorsey announced that he was going to donate a big share of his stocks to an employee pool to reward his employees. Dorsey is developing new products every week. When all technology stocks were going down, Twitter rose sharply. By the last week of October, the open interest (all available) options on twitter was higher than any other stock in the market- even more than Apple! Earnings call show that they are on the right path by increasing users and revenue and cutting costs. After moving up sharply to $31.36 on 10/27/15, the price dropped to $28.46 on 10/30/15; apart from my stock holdings I am took a wild bet on Twitter by buying call options (strike price: $50, expiry date : 3/18/16) for 14 cents each. If Twitter rise to $50, my options would have a value around $4; that is a 2,757% gain in less than 6 months!! On the other hand if Twitter goes up to its 10/27/15 high of $31.36, I would be able to sell my options at 33 cents (more than a 100% gain). I am not implying that Twitter would go up to $50 by 3/18/16 but intuitively I know that it might double within the next 3 years.

General Motors Company (GM)

Current Price: $31.62

Initial Purchase: 8/25/15, buy 10 shares at $24.62

Current recommendation: Hold till price drops below $25 and buy 10 shares.

Gain: 28.43% in 281 days.

As analysts have been expecting it was announced that auto sales have peaked. Car sales for some automakers were down as much as 30%. Due to low oil prices, most of the demand is for SUVs and trucks-globally. Hedge funds are getting out of GM. On 5/11/16, GM announced that it has finally turned a corner in Europe. Even though we cannot expect growth from these automakers, the auto market is expected to remain stable and profitable for a long time to come. GM is a PE of 5 and a yield around 5%, the stock is a safe place to park your money.

From last month

This is a really good value stock now. Now trading close to book value! Given the increased revenue projections, high dividend (5.4%), increased stock buybacks announced in January 2016 makes this a great buy so increase the holding when the price drops below $25.

Auto revenue would set a record for 2015. Most analysts believe that this trend cannot last and 2016 would not be so friendly for the autos. However what was pleasantly surprising was that as it happened with the US economy since 2009, in the Eurozone, the auto industry is doing very well. This is a sign that the European economy is on the rebound. Interest rates going up in the US and the rising US dollar is not good for the US car industry but rising employment and wages in the US would drive up demand. As of 12/1/15, GM P/E at 13 and Ford P/E at 12, these are cheap stocks.

With a 4.93% yield on 9/5/15, this is a steal! Now let us assume that the market is in a bear market and GM goes down to $15 per share; that would raise the yield to 9.8% while the10 year US Treasury is 2.13%. When investors get rational, they will chase after these high dividend stocks with long term growth prospect where you get paid to be patient.

Ford Motor Co (Symbol: F)

Current Price: $13.56

Initial Purchase: 8/24/15, buy 10 shares at $10.44

Current recommendation: Hold till price drops below $11 and buy 25 shares

Average cost with this purchase: $10.44 per share

Gain: 29.89% in 281 days!!

As analysts have been expecting it was announced that auto sales have peaked. Car sales for some automakers were down as much as 30%. Due to low oil prices, most of the demand is for SUVs and trucks-globally. Hedge funds are getting out of GM. On 5/11/16, GM announced that it has finally turned a corner in Europe. Even though we cannot expect growth from these automakers, the auto market is expected to remain stable and profitable for a long time to come. GM is a PE of 5 and a yield around 5%, the stock is a safe place to park your money.

From last month:

Currently the stock market is going through a correction (or a bear market). Now everyone is in fear so it is a time to nibble a little bit-if we see our price targets in the market. As Warren Buffet says, "Buy when others are fearful and sell when others are greedy". Please be forewarned that we could lose 25% to 66% in a bear phase and this could take many months or years; and that is the worst case scenario but very unlikely. Even during a bear market, we see market rallies.

As of 1/9/16, the dividend yield on Ford is at 4.78% and if the share price drops to $11, this yield will go up to 5.45%. and if the price drops to $9, the yield goes up to 6.67%! When the 10 year Treasury has yield of 2.5% or so, buying GM is a no brainer for the long term. Ford withstood the 2008 recession without a bailout from the government which shows that they are very strong when it comes to management.

Auto revenue would set a record for 2015. Most analysts believe that this trend cannot last and 2016 would not be so friendly for the autos. However what was pleasantly surprising was that as it happened with the US economy since 2009, in the Eurozone, the auto industry is doing very well. This is a sign that the European economy is on the rebound. Interest rates going up in the US and the rising US dollar is not good for the US car industry but rising employment and wages in the US would drive up demand. As of 12/1/15, GM P/E at 13 and Ford P/E at 12, these are cheap stocks.

Ford had a spectacular month in September (2015) with auto sales up 23% from last year! If we can keep the US economy humming along and see a recovery in the European economy, Ford should do okay in the long run.

In the stock market, for individual stocks as well as the market as a whole, the regulators have put in 'circuit breakers'. This was initially started after the 1987 crash. When a certain stock or the market moves up or down fast, these circuit breakers can come in to effect. At times, they can do more harm than good. They come in to effect at 7%, 13% and at 20%. If the Market goes down 20%, the whole market is closed for the day. On 8/24/15, when Dow fell 1100 points, 'panic selling' followed by 'panic buying', the circuit breakers came in to effect on Ford, only on the UP side or else Ford would have gone up more on the worst day for the market in 8 years!

General Electric (Symbol: GE)

Current Price: $30.34

Initial recommendation: 8/24/15, buy 10 shares at $19.37

Current recommendation: Hold till price drops below $25 and buy 25 shares.

Average cost with this purchase: $19.37 per share

Gain: 56.65% in 281 days!

From last month:

On 3/23/16- It was announced that the digital business is just getting started so the stock has a long way to go. This week GE hit an all-time high since 2008. This is not the old GE we used to know and I expect GE to be a growth stock in the future.

Since the market started crashing after 1/1/16, GE started moving lower but on 12/31/15, GE was at $31.49 and on 12/31/15, we had a gain of 62.57% in 129 days! S&P500 had a flat year for 2015 and the 10 year Treasury yield is at 2.5% or so. With all this volatility in the global financial markets, GE could go down to $20 or so but I expect GE to be around $40 or more by 1/1/18.

Out of all the shorts that increased from 9/30/15 to 10/15/15, GE was the 3rd highest, so no wonder GE went to a 7 year high. If I heard anyone saying that GE could go up by 49% in 90 days in 2015, no one would have believed it. It has been stick in the mud for more than 8 years. After the financial crisis, some thought that GE (only original Dow30) would even get dropped off the Dw30. It is so big, it rarely moves. As I stated on 10/5/15 (1st addendum for October 2015), I sold my $27 calls at a 300% profit but my intuition told me not to sell at that time. If I waited just 2 more days I would have got a 2,000% profit but the decision I made was a rational as GE hit a 3 year high and my options were going to expire in 2 months. What I had to say about GE on 10/5/15 (in my addendum:

General Electric (GE) was the biggest story today! For the past few years everyone thought I was crazy to recommend GE. As I have been saying they are going through a death and rebirth process. The new GE is going to be totally different than the GE of the past. Alan Peltz who owns the Hedge Fund TRIAN invested $2.5B in GE. The Chief Investment Officer of Trian stated that they consider GE to be totally 'risk free' with dividend yield close to 4% while the US 10 year treasury rate is at 1.99%. They are pressuring GE to increase their buybacks from $90B to $120B. Jim Cramer said that the price of GE could double with Trian getting in to GE. Trian expect margins to grow rapidly at GE. Now Trian is the #10 owner of GE and they see GE going up by 70%. I had GE stocks and call options. Maybe it was too premature but I sold my call options (GE, strike price $27, expiry: Jan 2016) at a 300% profit and kept the stocks. If GE goes to $54 as Jim Cramer predicts and if that happens prior to 1/15/16, I could have made a 10,000% profit but with options, one cannot take that risk. Next time GE goes down, I *will get in to options again. Over the past year or so, it has been trading between $24 and $26. It has been a trader's dream.*

19% of GE revenue comes from oil and China so the market tends to bring down the share price of GE in the short run giving us a buying opportunity. Per Barron's, of 8/29/15, "GE at about $25 isn't cheap at 19 times estimated 2015 earnings but profits could grow at double digit rates in coming years as it aims to create what it calls a focused infrastructure and technology company with 90% of earnings coming from industrial business by 2018".

Exxon Mobil Corporation (XOM)

Current Price: $90.20

Initial recommendation: 8/24/15, buy 4 shares at $66.55

Current recommendation: Hold till price drops to $65 and buy 6 shares.

Average cost with this purchase: $66.55 per share

Gain: 35.54% within 281 days!

On 4/26/16, after 6 decades, Exxon lost their AAA rating downgraded to AA+ - due to its debt level and refusal to cut the dividends. On 4/30/16, despite losses, Exxon raised its dividends by 2.7%-slimmest hike in 30 years.

From Last month:

On 3/8/16, the CEO of Chevron addressed analysts and stated the following: (1) They are going to cut capital expenditures (2) They will increase dividends (3) They will increase production. On 3/10/16, Paul Sankey of Wolfe Research stated that Chevron is a better buy than Exxon. Exxon has losses in Russia. Chevron will cut capital expenses by 50% from peak so the dividend is safe and sustainable.

Chevron need not make any acquisitions to make money in the future but hat is not true for Exxon. Most good assets of other companies are overpriced as they are expecting Exxon to go on a buying spree. No risk to the dividend at Exxon either. Exxon also have problems in the Middle East. Companies close to insolvency have assets (oil fields) that are not that attractive to buyers like Exxon.

On 2/16/16, an analyst announced that he expects the credit agencies to cut ratings for Exxon in 2016. Due to their large refinery business they are not very sensitive to changes in crude oil prices. After lifting of the oil and gas export ban, for the first time, there was a shipment of liquid natural gas from the US to Brazil on 2/24/16 and this was done by the only company that has the capacity to do it- Cheniere Energy (LNG). Carl Icahn is one of the major shareholders of Cheniere. Since Exxon is a major player in this area some think that they might even buy Cheniere in the future. On 3/2/16, the CEO of Exxon Mobil made these announcements:

- No more layoffs in 2016.
- He intends to increase the dividend as he wants the investors to hold the stock for a long time.
- He did NOT borrow $10 Billion to pay dividends or buyback stocks; even though they temporarily stopped the stock buyback program.
- Exxon Mobil has collected a 'war chest" of $30 Billion to go on a future buying binge. Per analyst, Doug Terreson of Evercore, their balance sheet is only second to J&J and crude oil (WTI) has to go down $15 and stay there for long for Exxon and Chevron to cut their dividends.

Best oil analyst, Doug Terreson of Evercore, on 2/1/16 stated that they expect the best in oil to come from Exxon, Chevron and BP. He thinks that the dividend is safe. Between 1/1/16 and 2/15/16, the stock market (S&P 500) declined by 8.71%; during the same time Exxon Mobil went UP by 4.65%. It was announced on CNBC on 2/8/16 that when hedge funds want exposure to oil, they invest in Exxon Mobil. On 2/2/16, Exxon stopped its buyback plan for the first time in 15 years as its earnings went down by 60%. BP earnings declined by 91% and stock price declined by 9%. 2/12/16 was the best day in 7 years for crude oil as it rose by 10.7%. Experts believe the bottom for petroleum was already reached and bottom for crude would be reached within the next 60 days.

What Goldman Sachs predicted many months ago is finally happening. A barrel of oil is below $35 and most say that it could go below $20 as there is no room for storage anymore and supply exceed the demand. Saudis are operating at full capacity and they have no incentive to cut production to benefit others. However tensions are rising in the Middle East so that could upset the apple cart. Surprisingly when tensions rose between Iran and Saudis as they got close to a face to face war, the price of oil did not go up at all. One year ago, that would have sent the price of oil sky high. Experts are divided on the future prices of oil. Some say 'low for long' while others say that we are close to a bottom and then prices would shoot up soon. Prices always over shoot so I think that when most small fracking companies go insolvent, when the over supply problem gets resolved, as demand grows we might see a rapid increase in the price. In December 2015, Republican Party agreed to extend the credit for solar energy so as to get President Obama to agree to lift the 40 year ban on crude oil. I think that this is a mistake for the long term. Due to this lifting of the ban, now there is no difference between WTI and Brent (US and International prices). If this is true for natural gas, as there is a huge variance between the prices we pay for it and what it costs in other countries, in the years to come, most people in cold states will have a problem paying for heating bills. On 1/6/15, T.Boone Pickens was on CNBC Mad Money and he said that this price decline is solely due to an over-supply problem but the supply exceed the demand only by 1 million barrels per day when in the 1980s when we had the problem, we had an over-supply of 20 million barrels per day. Also the demand is growing as European economy keeps growing and US consumers are going back to gas inefficient vehicles. Pickens is predicting the price of a barrel of oil rising to $70 by year end. John Dowd, who manages Fidelity Select Energy Portfolio wants to invest in oil companies with strong balance sheets who can manage themselves well whatever happens to the price of oil. Exon Mobil is his top holding (or 12.4% of his portfolio. Other companies on his portfolio includes Schluberger (7.9%), EOG (6.6%) Valero (5%) and Chevron (4.8%). Between 8/24/15 (market crash) and 11/3/15, Exxon rose by 18% and Chevron rose by 40%; even the oil prices going below $35 did not bring these share prices to the 8/24/15 level. Therefore it is extremely likely that we could see Exxon and Chevron going down sharply soon but in about 2 years we would be able to reap the rewards. This is why I want to add Chevron and start nibbling at it now so we could lower the average cost in the future by buying more when the price drops further.

On 11/13/15, CNBC reported that an unnamed person or an entity bought put options on Exxon worth $6 million assuming that the share price of Exxon would drop to $60 over the next 3 months. First of all, I do not think that would happen as Exxon has a strong balance sheet and there are ways that they can benefit even from low oil prices (i.e. refineries). Price of oil could go down in the short run and stay down for a while the commodity future prices should come down and that would stop hedge funds being heavily involved in oil; and this should lead to a bottom of the oil price. Also the Middle East situation could lead to higher prices due to geopolitical instability. On the other hand, if the share price drops to $60, that would be an excellent buying opportunity. Furthermore with all the people shorting the stock, we might see the share price shoot up when they run to cover their shorts.

As with Twitter, when I recommended Exxon, it was hated by everyone on Wall Street and there were many who even doubted that they would keep their dividend intact. Then as I stated last month, technical analysis showed that professionals were buying Exxon in big numbers. On 10/30/15, Exxon and Chevron had their earning calls and they both beat Wall Street 2015 Q3 estimates. Also Chevron announced a 50% reduction in their costs. Exxon cash position was very good and 50% of that was spent on dividends. Chevron's cash flow will get positive in 2016. Experts believe that since these are integrated oil companies, they are not so affected by oil prices so when oil prices go up, they will not benefit as so some other oil or fracking companies; however I have seen a direct link between oil prices and the share price of Exxon. Now it is up 24.33% within 91 days so it is quite possible that it might go down in the near future; if that happens, consider it as a buying opportunity. I am confident that it would reach its old all-time high of $100 within the next 3 years. Even after that this is a good stock to hold for decades.

The energy sector is in a massive bear market and a recession; with revenues declining 60%+ per quarter and even with that back drop, our Exxon Mobil managed to gain 14% in 30 days. On Jim Cramer's segment on "off the charts" on 9/29/15, the technician who studied the chart of Exxon shows that the price is bottoming out as she can see a 'positive divergence' (chartist lingo!) also she could see 'Aroon'(a name technicians have taken from Sanskrit to say 'dawn's early light). Studying of charts and technical analysis is much more important than fundamental analysis (demand/supply, valuations etc.) in predicting the future of a stock, commodity or a market. If you put make your fundamental analysis as your # 1 priority, it is like putting the cart before the horse. I have seen the truth of this statement during the past 30 years. These technical indicators are showing that big funds are now getting very interested in Exxon. Don't forget that 2 months ago when they all hated Exxon and stated in my newsletter that I am in love with Exxon and strongly urged you to start nibbling at it.

I am in love with Exxon Mobil! Then why am I asking you to purchase only nibble at 4 shares for now? Strategy to bring down the long term average cost. The dividend rate (yield) on 8/23/15 is at 2.9%. Not only this is a stellar company but it is totally devoted to their investors and more importantly to their dividend payout. If the price drops to $36, the yield goes up to 5.8%.Imagine all the institutions that would get attracted to this stock. What happens if WTI goes over $100 as a few oil men expect it to happen?

I like going against the herd. In fact, this is 'bluest of the bluest' stocks in an industry that many believe that they are headed for Armageddon. I am talking of Exxon Mobile (XOM). I just cannot praise this stock enough but start nibbling with the expectation that it might continue to go down for the next 5 years. There is a high probability that it might turnaround in 12 to 18 months but if you do not expect it, you will not get disappointed. This is the giant of the giants. It reached its all-time high of $100 on 4/1/14. So now it is down 28% to $72. It is right at the simple moving average so in the near future, it could down drastically. Most probably this is something you can keep in your portfolio for the next 30 to 50 years. Periodically you have to check to see if there is something drastic coming down the pipeline and sell it but I am confident that Exxon Mobile would be able to adjust to changes and keep prospering. A few months ago, an analyst on CNBC was showing that all these big oil companies were making so little money now that their 'earnings per share' was less than the expected 'dividend per share'; and he concluded that all oil companies would freeze their dividend this year. Most, including Chevron and Shell did that. Not only Exxon Mobile paid a dividend, it also increased it (by a little bit). I personally checked their dividend history and found that every single year since 1911, they paid out a dividend! Not only that, for the past 32 years, each year, they have been increasing the dividend by an average rate of 6.4%! So I bet that they want to keep this reputation or else it would have been to their benefit to freeze the dividend and increase their cash position to get ready to buy all the hundreds of oil companies that will declare bankruptcy within the next 12 months. In the 70's GM had that reputation about paying out annual dividends. Hopefully what happened to GM will not happen to Exxon Mobile. Out of the original Dow 30, only GE is there today. In the 2007 recession, they came close to getting themselves out of the Dow30. So this shows that Exxon Mobile is not a sure thing. If you want a sure thing, buy US treasuries and get 2% per year. Some bozo called Donald Trump introduced you to 'the art of the deal'; now let me introduce you to 'the art of nibbling'. The current price of XOM is at $72. Let us say you buy 10 shares (or multiples of 10 shares) now and each time the share price goes down by another 10% by another 10 shares (or multiples of 10 shares). According to this example, if XOM goes down to $10, you would have accumulated 180 shares of XOM for the total cost of $6,227.39(plus commission). Now your average cost is $34.60! Now let us assume that kept the current dividend in terms of dollars and it took 5 years for the price to drop from $72 to $10 (which is extremely unlikely) and you purchased 36 shares per year. Believe it or not, according to these assumptions, over the 5 years, you would have received $1,598.40 in total dividends. If you factor the dividend, your total cost goes down to $4,629 and the average cost goes down to $25.72-even though the stock itself went down by 85%. Now that is Part 1 of the 'art of nibbling'(which I just developed this week-up to this point I did not have it as a science). Now let us assume that over the next 10 years, with the dividend increasing 6% per year as they have done for the past 32 years, the share price increased 30% per year to get the price to $149-this is not unrealistic after such a rapid drop and only a 49% move up from 4/1/14. Then for that 10 year period you would have received $7,976.79 in dividends alone. Your XOM holding would be worth $ 26,824.51. Remember that during the first 5 years, your net cost was $4,629.00. If you reinvest your dividends in XOM and taking the compounded dividend and rate of growth, the potential to make money is higher. This is just an example by making so many assumptions but I was trying to create a general picture in your mind. To be realistic, I do not think that XOM will go down to $10 and it will go down for 5 years. Most probably it will start going up next year and it will hit $150 within 2 years and it will keep on increasing dividends for the next 10 years. Since the increase was less than 6% this year, they might increase it more next year to get back to the average of 6%. I already bought my first 'nibble'.

Chevron (CVX)

Current Price: $102.28

Initial recommendation: Buy 2 shares at $79.66 on 1/10/16

Current recommendation: If the price drops below $75, purchase 3 more shares

Average cost with this purchase: $79.66

Gain: 28.22% within 142 days!

From last month:

On 3/8/16, the CEO of Chevron addressed analysts and stated the following: (1) They are going to cut capital expenditures (2) They will increase dividends (3) They will increase production. On 3/10/16, Paul Sankey of Wolfe Research stated that Chevron is a better buy than Exxon. Exxon has losses in Russia. Chevron will cut capital expenses by 50% from peak so the dividend is safe and sustainable. Chevron need not make any acquisitions to make money in the future but hat is not true for Exxon. Most good assets of other companies are overpriced as they are expecting Exxon to go on a buying spree. No risk to the dividend at Exxon either. Exxon also have problems in the Middle East. Companies close to insolvency have assets (oil fields) that are not that attractive to buyers like Exxon.

On 1/29/16 Chevron reported its first loss since 2002- $0.31 per share; but after extraordinary items, the loss was $0.26 per share.

Ratings on Chevron was reduced from AA to AA-. For the moment, there is no risk of losing the high dividends but if oil stays down for long, that risk will keep getting higher. Best oil analyst, Doug Terreson of Evercore, on 2/1/16 stated that they expect the best in oil to come from Exxon, Chevron and BP. He thinks that the dividend is safe. 2/12/16 was the best day in 7 years for crude oil as it rose by 10.7%. Experts believe the bottom for petroleum was already reached and bottom for crude would be reached within the next 60 days.

What Goldman Sachs predicted many months ago is finally happening. A barrel of oil is below $35 and most say that it could go below $20 as there is no room for storage anymore and supply exceed the demand. Saudis are operating at full capacity and they have no incentive to cut production to benefit others. However tensions are rising in the Middle East so that could upset the apple cart. Surprisingly when tensions rose between Iran and Saudis as they got close to a face to face war, the price of oil did not go up at all. One year ago, that would have sent the price of oil sky high. Experts are divided on the future prices of oil. Some say 'low for long' while others say that we are close to a bottom and then prices would shoot up soon. Prices always over shoot so I think that when most small fracking companies go insolvent, when the over supply problem gets resolved, as demand grows we might see a rapid increase in the price. In December 2015, Republican Party agreed to extend the credit for solar energy so as to get President Obama to agree to lift the 40 year ban on crude oil. I think that this is a mistake for the long term. Due to this lifting of the ban, now there is no difference between WTI and Brent (US and International prices). If this is true for natural gas, as there is a huge variance between the prices we pay for it and what it costs in other countries, in the years to come, most people in cold states will have a problem paying for heating bills. On 1/6/15, T.Boone Pickens was on CNBC Mad Money and he said that this price decline is solely due to an over-supply problem but the supply exceed the demand only by 1 million barrels per day when in the 1980s when we had the problem, we had an over-supply of 20 million barrels per day. Also the demand is growing as European economy keeps growing and US consumers are going back to gas inefficient vehicles. Pickens is predicting the price of a barrel of oil rising to $70 by year end. John Dowd, who manages Fidelity Select Energy Portfolio wants to invest in oil companies with strong balance sheets who can manage themselves well whatever happens to the price of oil. Exon Mobil is his top holding (or 12.4% of his portfolio. Other companies on his portfolio includes Schluberger (7.9%), EOG (6.6%) Valero (5%) and Chevron (4.8%). Between 8/24/15 (market crash) and 11/3/15, Exxon rose by 18% and Chevron rose by 40%; even the oil prices going below $35 did not bring these share prices to the 8/24/15 level. Therefore it is extremely likely that we could see Exxon and Chevron going down sharply soon but in about 2 years we would be able to reap the rewards. This is why I want to add Chevron and start nibbling at it now so we could lower the average cost in the future by buying more when the price drops further.

IBM (IBM)

Current Price: $153.81

Initial recommendation: 1/25/16, buy 2 shares at $121.64

Current recommendation: 1/25/16, buy 2 shares at $122 and when it goes under $110 buy 3 shares and another 3 when it goes under $100 and so on

Average cost $121.64

Gain: 26.45% in 127 days

From last month:

This has become a long term value stock. Some say it will never come back in style again. Warren Buffet keeps buying more and more share but this might have gone against IBM. Buffet must have forced them to pay dividends and buyback shares when they could have bought other technology companies and grown exponentially. It is down from an all-time high of $213. It might take a long time to recover but it pays to wait with a 4.3% dividend.

Schlumberger Limited (SLB)-

Current Price: $77.60

Initial recommendation: 1/25/16, buy 2 shares at $63.23

Current recommendation: 1/25/16, buy 2 shares at $63.23 and 2 more shares when it drops below $50, and let us keep buying as the price declines so when it goes down to $14, we can buy about 1,000 shares.

Average cost $63.23

Gain: 22.73 % in 127 days!

According to Bloomberg News, on 5/24/16, Goldman Sachs after being bearish on oil for years, added Schlumberger to its conviction buy list. Analyst Waqar Syed reiterated a $94 price target- nearly 30% above the stock price of 5/24/16.

From last month:

This is a time to nibble at good oil companies as it is expected that oil process would bottom in 2016 and there is a good possibility that oil would sky rocket within the next 2 years.

Valley National Bancorp (VLY)

Current Price: $9.61

Initial recommendation: 1/19/16, buy 5 shares at $8.59

Current recommendation: 1/19/16, buy 5 shares at $8.59 on 1/19/16; and then if the price drops below $6, buy 25 shares

Average cost with this purchase: $8.59

Gain: 11.87% in 133 days.

From last month:

Valley National Bancorp (VLY)

- This is very different from my other sections. This is a small cap bank with $2.1Billion. On 1/15/16, the stock closed at $8.68 with a dividend yield of 4.98%.
- Valley National Bancorp operates as the holding company for the Valley National Bank that provides commercial, retail, insurance, and wealth management financial services products. As of December 31, 2014, it operated 224 branches in northern and central New Jersey; the New York City boroughs of Manhattan, Brooklyn, Queens, and Long Island; and southeast and central Florida. The company was founded in 1927 and is headquartered in Wayne, New Jersey

- Initially buy 5 shares of VLY at $8.68 or the lowest possible price on 1/19/16. If the price drops below $6, buy 25 shares.

iShares MSCI Canada (EWC)

Current Price: $24.82

Initial recommendation: 1/19/16, buy 3 shares at $18.68

Current recommendation: 1/19/16, buy 3 shares at $18.68 on 1/19/16; and then if the price drops below $16, buy 7 shares

Average cost with this purchase: $18.68

Gain: 32.87% in 133days!!

From last month:

iShares MSCI Canada (symbol: EWC)

- The Fund Summary-The investment seeks to track the investment results of the MSCI Canada Index. The fund will at all times invest at least 90% of its assets in the securities of its underlying index and in depositary receipts representing securities in its underlying index. The underlying index may include large-, mid- or small-capitalization companies. Components of the underlying index primarily include energy, financials and materials companies.
- Canadian economy and markets are deeply connected to the oil industry. Oil and gas companies make up 20 to **30%** of the value of the Toronto Stock Exchange (TSX), One way to invest in the future rises in the oil

sector is to buy in to the stock market of Canada.

- This ETF, "EWC" has gone down from $32 on 7/31/14 to $18.97 on 1/15/16 which is a 40.72% decline in 17.5 months. There is a possibility that it could even go down to the technical support level of $8.60 (in 2002).

- At this time buy 3 shares at $19 or the lowest on 1/19/16. The strategy is to keep on buying as the price drops to have a very low average cost when the ETF starts to move up. For example if you buy 3 shares at $19, 7 shares at $15, 10 shares at $10 and 100 shares at $5, you will own 120 shares at an average cost of $6.35. In 3 years, when this ETF goes back to $32, you would have made a 403.94% profit!!

Bank of America Corporation (BAC)

Current Price: $15.05

Initial recommendation: Buy 5 shares at $14.94 on 1/10/16

Second recommendation: Buy 20 shares on 1/15/16 at $14.13

Third recommendation: Buy 10 shares on 2/16/16 at $12.11

Average cost with this purchase: 13.67

Gain: 10.10 % within 142 days.

From Last Month:

For years the market waited for the first rate increase by the Federal Reserve to buy bank stocks as normalization of rates is good for banks. So what happened? Even though banks in the US are safe, European banks are at risk. This dragged all bank stocks in the US too.

We are upgrading Bank of America to **Buy** from Hold. With Bank of America's (ticker: BAC) fourth-quarter results being in line with our expectation and no change to our next-12-months earnings-per-share estimate, we believe Bank of America's 7% share price decline over the last week is fundamentally unjustified. Fourth-quarter EPS were essentially in line with our expectations. Reported EPS of 28 cents beat our 26 cents estimate and consensus of 27 cents. After excluding unusual items we peg core EPS at 34 cents, which was modestly below our 35 cents forecast. Boosting energy-related credit reserves would only have a modest impact on EPS. Energy-related credit reserves ended 2015 at approximately $500 million, which represents roughly 2.3% of Bank of America's $21.3 billion of energy-related loans. While this is significantly below some of its peers (e.g., Wells Fargo (WFC) and U.S. Bancorp (USB) has disclosed energy-related reserve coverage ratios of 7.1% and 5.4%, respectively), it is not terribly surprising given the level of disclosed energy related provisioning in 2015. While additional energy-related reserve builds are likely in the first half, the builds may not be extremely large as management believes an oil price of $30 per barrel for nine quarters would drive incremental losses of $700 million. However, even if significant oil-related reserve builds prove necessary in 2016 we would expect a modest net impact on EPS. Additional reserve builds of approximately $1.0 billion would push Bank of America's energy-related credit reserve ratio north of 7% and only reduce 2016 EPS by approximately six cents (less than 4% of the $1.55 consensus 2016 EPS estimate). Total loan balances increased for a third consecutive quarter. While full year loan growth was a relatively modest 2.5%, Bank of America turned an important corner in 2015 as core loan growth finally eclipsed ongoing contraction in the runoff loan portfolio. We believe that the ability to continue delivering loan growth will be important as Bank of America seeks to accelerate revenue growth in a still challenged operating environment.(Sandler O Neil, Barrons, 1/20/16).

The Walt Disney Company (DIS)

Current Price: $99.89

Initial recommendation: Buy 2 shares at $98.50 on 1/10/16

Second recommendation: Buy 3 shares on 2/16/16 at $91.79

Average cost with this purchase: $94.47

Gain: 5.74 % in 142 days

From Last Month:

Even with Star Wars movie, Disney has been on the decline. Interestingly the day the movie came out, an analyst came with a downgrade and the share price started declining again. Why? All the pessimism is about declining earnings at ESPN. I do not think that this is serious at all. I have confidence in Disney management with one of the greatest CEOs. On 11/20/15, the share price was at $120 so this is a good indicator of what kind of growth we could expect from Disney in the future. We might see the price declining for 6 to 12 months giving us a chance to decrease the average cost of our purchases.

Alcoa Inc. (AA)

Current Price: $9.48

Initial recommendation: 8/24/15, buy 10 shares at $7.97

Current recommendation: Hold till price drops under $6 and buy 20 shares

Average cost with this purchase: $7.97 per share

Gain: 18.95% in 281 days

From Last Month:

This too we purchased for the long run expecting a price decline in the short run so we could accumulate more share and reduce the average cost. However with the changes made by the current management and with the prospect of splitting the company in to two-commodity part and the engineering part, the prospects for Alcoa are excellent. If the price drops below $8, purchase more shares.

Apple Inc. (AAPL)

Current Price: $100.40 (as of 5/31/16)

Initial recommendation: 8/24/15, buy 3 shares at $92

2nd recommendation: 1/11/16, buy 6 shares at $96.96

May 2016 purchases: 5/2/16; 5@ $92.40 and on 5/12/16; 5@ $89.47

Current recommendation:

Average cost with this purchase: $93.01 per share (as of 5/12/16)

Gain: 7.95% within 281 days

Right now this has the biggest risk and the biggest reward. "No risk, no reward". Day by day, the nay sayers are growing. More and more, pundits are saying that Apple will take the same road as Nokia, Xerox and Eastman Kodak (or even IBM). Latest is that Apple will take 3 years and not 2 to come up with a major change in the IPhone. Shark Tank's billionaire Kevin O'Leary who used to be a big fan of Apple for years and who also started his own ETFs known as O'Shares states that his new Samsung can do everything but wash his laundry and it will take ages for Apple to come to that stage. The most bearish people on Apple expect the share price to hit $85 by the latter part of 2016. To me, that is not bad at all. It hit $89 in May 2016. If it goes to $85, I suggest you buy 5 more shares and another 5 shares at $75. Carl Icahn got in to Apple years ago when it was a dud and he got

Apple to be more shareholder friendly. During the past few weeks, he sold all his Apple holdings with a net profit of $4 Billion! Carl was worried that Apple might have more problems in China. In fact, one year ago, Carl said that he will never sell Apple. Then should everyone get out of Apple too? No, not by a long shot. I still have faith in Apple and more than that the greatest investor this world has ever known and the 2nd most richest man on Earth, Warren Buffet just bought $1 billion in Apple shares! For many decades, he avoided technology stocks till he got in to IBM which has been a dud for the longest time. IBM too is showing signs of turning around. On 5/12/16, Apple dropped below $90 for the first time in 2 years giving us another chance to increase our stake in Apple; also after a long time they dropped below Google aka Alphabet in market cap to $496B. On 5/13/16, Apple announced that they were going to invest $1B in China. Their profit margin is at 23% while the profit margin for their competitors is around 7% which could lead to a bigger problem for Apple. Apple makes a big deal about going in to India for the first time and how India is going to take over China as the most populated country; however keep in mind that per capita income of India (GDP/# of people) is US $1,500 per year and the monthly average wage in India is US $295. I cannot see a mad rush to buy a $700 IPhones. People will kill each other to steal an IPhone! On 5/2/16, Tim Cook, CEO of Apple, on CNBC show Mad Money stated the following:

- In China, other smart phone users turning to Apple is huge.
- In 2 years, Apple grew 70% in China.
- The middle class in China is growing from 50 million to 500 million in 5 years.
- India will be the most populous country in 2020 and most young people in India wants to own a smart phone.

From Last month

On 4/30/16, Apple announced that it would cut $2B in IPhone inventories. Last week Apple raised its dividends by 10% to 57 cents per share-total dividends paid by Apple is at $12.6B which is 3.21% of all dividends paid by the S&P500 companies. This makes Apple the biggest payer of dividends overtaking Exxon Mobil. Apple earnings went down by 22% and they missed revenue guidelines. First sales drop in 13 years! Sold 12 million watches. Their IPhones fetch a margin of around 40% when others have a margin of around 0. On 4/26/16, Per Toni Saccibaughi of Sanford Bernstein analyst Apple product cycle will come in September 2016 so the stock will start going up July 2016. Only 60% of handsets in the world are smartphones. Apple just entered the market in India and in a few years India will overtake China as the most populated country on Earth. Per Barron's article on Apple on 4/9/16:

- Stock could rise to $150 in 12 months
- Current pessimism due to slowing growth of IPhone sales that account for 2/3 of revenue
- Total revenue projected to decline by 2.4% to $228.1B pulling profits down by 6.3% to $50B.
- Apple service already brings in 15% of Gross Profit., and could reach 29% by 2020.
- Apple has a long term potential to reach 1.5b active devices with stable free cash flow if $67B a year up from a 1B devices now and $56B in free cash projected for this year.

From last month:

First of all I want to apologize for stating that the cash position of Apple is $20B; it is really $200B-worldwide and mostly in other countries. On 1/27/16, Professor Damodoran, expert on value stocks, reported that according to his Apple is no longer a growth company but a value company. Yet people are still trading Apple like a growth company. As Prof. Damodoran put it, "People are addicted to IPhones so it is like the cigarette stock Altria/Phillip Morris. At $95 it is a great buy as it has the mother of all balance sheets".

Apple- As I have stated before, for many years all of Wall Street loved Apple and then a couple of months ago, all on Wall Street started hating Apple. Earnings estimates kept going down. At that time I asked you to start nibbling (buying) Apple. Last week 2 major firms issued buy recommendations on Apple. Where were they when I asked you to buy Apple? On 1/19/16, Goldman Sachs gave a buy recommendation on Apple with a future price target of $150. On 1/22/16, Gene Munster of Piper Jeffries came out with a buy recommendation on Apple with a price target of $150 in 9 months and on that day alone Apple went up by 5%. On 1/20/16, Apple hit an intraday low of $93.42 and rose to $101.42 on 1/22/16. If Apple goes to $150 in 9 months, from the low of 1/20/16, it is a 61% gain in 9 months in one of the most valuable and the biggest company in the world. Scott Kessler of S&P Capital IQ issued a very strong buy recommendation on Apple. For the past year or so everyone in the market knew that Apple was stealing employees from Tesla and as with everything else they were secretly working on a car. Elan Musk used to joke that Apple hires their fired employees. Around 1/20/16,

Elan Musk stated that Apple is developing their own car. Some say that Apple should buy Tesla but Elan Musk may not be willing to sell Tesla. I personally do not think that Elan Musk would be able to stand in the way of Apple if they decide to have a hostile takeover. All insiders and 5%+ owners own only 22% of Tesla. Tesla is extremely over-valued but their market cap is at $26.5Billion and Apple's Cash and Short Term Investments come to about $50Billion and you add Net AR and you get about $80 Billion. Can Apple buy Tesla? You do the math! In my opinion, Apple should wait for a stock market crash or the bear to make a dent in stock prices where Tesla market cap drops to about $12 Billion and then make a hostile takeover. The guy in charge of the car division at Apple resigned around 1/22/16

Market experts are confused about Apple. Some long term believers have begun to sell Apple. I am a firm believer in Apple. Now this is a mature company with a low P/E and a respectable yield. When they get in to the auto business and come up with other new products, there will be resurgence. With all the cash on their balance sheet, they should be able to make some good acquisitions.

As I mentioned a few weeks ago, in my addendums, Apple had the highest short sell increase and I predicted that this will cause the price of Apple to go up as these people will have to do some panic buying to cover their shorts; and as I predicted within the past 3 weeks, Apple rose from $110 to $120 (9% in 3 weeks). On 10/22/15, Brad Lamensdorf who predicts a bear market in 2016 and who was shorting Apple said that they got out of the Apple short position. However Brad was bullish for the US market for 2015 Q4. On 10/11/15, in my 2nd addendum, this is what I had to say about Apple:

As I have been saying in the past, on Wall Street, love can turn in to hate in an instant. A month or two ago (or prior), it was impossible to find someone who did not love Apple on Wall Street. Now almost everyone hates Apple. Kevin O' Leary, Shark Tanks Billionaire who thinks he is an expert on stocks was saying that Twitter was dead prior to its astronomical rise of the stock also mentioned that Apple has no future now. Why? His 18 year old son told him that he hates Apple music. How stupid! For the past year or so he would come on TV and say that Apple was the best stock ever. On 8/25/15, when the market crashed 1100 points, Apple CEO emailed Jim Cramer of CNBC to let him know that IPhone sales are growing rapidly in China and that is what stopped the carnage-not limited to Apple. Recently Nike earnings report also show that China sales are doing great. Why? These American products are status symbols for the Chinese. As I said a few days ago, Apple had the highest short interest hike of all stocks with a rise of 14 million in one week. When I was talking about all the stocks that went up sharply last week due to short coverings, did you wish you were able to buy them prior to that rise? Now here you have that with Apple. Next time Apple would report earnings would be on 10/27/15. There is a very high probability that Apple would skyrocket around 10/27/15. I looked at call option prices but they are too rich for my blood but this means you can make a lot of money by writing options on Apple.

We buy stocks for the long run and this is a stellar stock as well as the biggest company (per market cap) in the world. Once again, Carl Icahn was on CNBC and he said that he is divided about buying more Apple now or waiting for a lower price but he said that buying more of Apple is a 'no brainer'. Every week, I watch short interest figures and I pay most attention to the highest increases in short positions. To my greatest surprise, for the week, 9/15/15-9/21/15, Apple was #1 with 13 million share increase of shorts! I watch these figures because it is highly likely that these stocks will get caught to short squeeze in the future and drive up the price of the stock in an insane manner. With a current PE of 12 and a dividend yield of 1.89%, Apple is a good buy for the long term.

4 GLOSSARY

- **ADR (American Depository Receipt)-** Certificate issued by a bank in the US representing a specified number of shares (or one share) in a foreign stock that is traded on a U.S. exchange.
- **Arbitrage-** practice of taking advantage of a price difference between two or more markets.
- **Balance Sheet-** Financial statement that covers assets, liabilities and equity of an entity.
- **Bear Market-** A market condition in which the prices of securities are falling. Some would define a bear market when the securities are down 20% from it's recent high.
- **Blue Chip Stock-** A stock of a well-established, financially sound company.
- **Book Value-**Value listed on the balance sheet
- **Bull Market-**A market condition in which the prices of securities are rising.
- **Contrarian-**Opposing the popular view
- **Credit Default Swap-**A credit default swap is a type of contract that offers a guarantee against the non-payment of a loan; usually issued by banks.
- **Credit Spread-** The spread between Treasury securities and non-Treasury securities that are identical in all respects except for quality rating.

- **Dividend**-see stock dividend
- **Dow Jones Industrial Average-** price-weighted average of 30 significant stocks traded on the New York Stock Exchange and the Nasdaq.
- **Earnings per share**-Earnings divided by the number of shares outstanding.
- **Emerging Markets-** An emerging market is a country that has some characteristics of a developed market, but does not meet standards to be a developed market.
- **Exchange Rate-** The price of a nation's currency in terms of another currency.
- **ETF (exchange traded fund)-** is a marketable security that tracks an index, a commodity, bonds, or a basket of assets like an index fund. Unlike mutual funds, an ETF trades like a common stock on a stock exchange.
- **Exercise of options**- the buyer (or holder) of a call contract may exercise his or her right to buy the underlying shares at the specified price (the strike price); the buyer of a put contract may exercise his or her right to sell the underlying shares at the agreed-upon price.
- **Expiration (of options)-** All options have a limited useful lifespan and every option contract is defined by an expiration month. The option expiration date is the date on which an options contract becomes invalid and the right to exercise it no longer exists. For many decades, the option expiration date was 3rd Friday of the month.
- **Ex Stock Dividend-** usually set for stocks two business days before the record date. If you purchase a stock on its ex-dividend date or after, you will not receive the next dividend payment

- **Federal Fund Rate-** The interest rate at which a depository institution lends funds maintained at the Federal Reserve to another depository institution overnight.
- **Federal Open Market Committee (FOMC)-** The monetary policymaking body of the Federal Reserve System. The FOMC is composed of 12 members--the seven members of the Board of Governors and five of the 12 Reserve Bank presidents.
- **Federal Reserve Bank-** the central banking system of the United States
- **401K plan-** A qualified plan established by employers to which eligible employees may make salary deferral (salary reduction) contributions on a post-tax and/or pretax basis.
- **Futures Market-** An auction market in which participants buy and sell commodity/future contracts for delivery on a specified future date.
- **GDP-** The total value of all goods and services produced within a country.
- **Going Public-** The process of selling shares that were formerly privately held to new investors for the first time.
- **Government Securities-**A bond (or debt obligation) issued by a government authority, with a promise of repayment upon maturity that is backed by said government.
- **Growth Funds-**The Growth Fund seeks to provide capital appreciation and some current income.
- **Hedging-**A risk management strategy used in limiting or offsetting probability of loss from fluctuations in the prices of commodities, currencies, bonds, stocks and so on.
- **Hedge Funds-** privately-owned companies that pool investors' dollars and reinvest them into all kinds of complicated financial instruments.

- **High Yield Bonds**-A high paying bond with a lower credit rating than investment-grade corporate bonds
- **Illegal Dividend**-A dividend declared by a corporation that is in violation of its charter and/or of state laws
- **Index Funds**-When an investor purchases a share of an index fund, he or she is purchasing a share of a portfolio that contains the securities in an underlying index.
- **Index Options**-Index options usually have a contract multiplier of $100, meaning that the price of an index option equals the quoted premium times $100. Unlike options in shares of stock or even commodities, it's not possible to physically deliver the underlying index to the purchaser of an index option
- **IRA Accounts**-Account at a financial institution that allows an individual to save for retirement with tax-free growth or on a tax-deferred basis
- **In the money (options)**- Situation in which an option's strike price is below the current market price of the underlier (for a call option) or above
- **Junk Bonds-**A security issued by a corporation that is considered to offer a high risk to bondholders
- **LEAPS (options)-** Long Term Equity AnticiPation Security Options are options of longer term until expiry than other, more common, options.
- **LBO (Leverage Buyouts)-** stands for Leveraged Buyout and refers to the takeover of a company that utilizes mainly debt to finance the buyout
- **Load Funds**-A mutual fund that comes with a sales charge or commission
- **Margin Accounts**-A brokerage account in which the broker lends the customer cash to purchase securities

- **Market to Market**-Refers to accounting for the value of an asset or liability based on the current market price instead of book value.
- **MLP (Master Limited Partnership)-** limited partnership that is publicly traded on an exchange
- **M1, M2, M3, M4** – see money supply
- **Money Supply**- Include cash, coins and balances held in checking & savings accounts. M1, also called narrow money, normally include coins and notes in circulation and other money equivalents that are easily convertible into cash. M2 includes M1 plus short-term time deposits in banks and 24-hour money market funds. M3 includes M2 plus longer-term time deposits and money market funds with more than 24-hour maturity. M4 includes M3 plus other deposits. The term broad money is used to describe M2, M3 or M4, depending on the local practice.
- **Money Market Funds**-One of the sections of a financial market where securities and financial instruments with short-term maturities are traded is called the money market.
- **Moving Averages**-A technical analysis term meaning the average price of a security over a specified time period.
- **Municipal Bonds**-A debt security issued by a state, municipality or county to finance its capital expenditures. Municipal bonds are exempt from federal taxes and from most state and local taxes, especially if you live in the state in which the bond is issued.
- **Mutual Funds**-An investment vehicle that is made up of a pool of funds collected from many investors for the purpose of investing in securities such as stocks, bonds, money market instruments and similar assets

- **Naked Options**-A trading position where the seller of an option contract does not own any, or enough, of the underlying security
- **NASDAQ**-created by the National Association of Securities Dealers (NASD) to enable investors to trade securities on a computerized, speedy and transparent system, and commenced operations on February 8, 1971.
- **NYSE**-A stock exchange based in New York City, which is considered the largest equities-based exchange in the world based on total market capitalization of its listed securities.
- **Net Asset Value**-A mutual fund's price per share or exchange-traded fund's (ETF) per-share value. In both cases, the per-share dollar amount of the fund is calculated by dividing the total value of all the securities in its portfolio, less any liabilities, by the number of fund shares outstanding
- **No Load Funds**-A mutual fund in which shares are sold without a commission or sales charge.
- **Off Balance Sheet Financing**-A form of financing in which large capital expenditures are kept off of a company's balance sheet through various classification methods. For anyone who was invested in Enron, off-balance sheet (OBS) financing is a scary term.
- **Offshore**-Located or based outside of one's national boundaries.

- **Open Market Operations**-Market interventions by a central bank to manipulate liquidity levels by buying or selling short term securities.
- **Options**-see Stock Options-

- **Out of the money (options)-** the strike price of the option exceeds the share price of the underlying equity.
- **OTC (Over the counter)-** A decentralized market, without a central physical location,
- **Penny Stocks-**common stock, usually highly speculative, selling for less than a dollar a share.
- **Preferred Stocks-** Dividends that are paid out prior common stock dividends are paid out.
- **Prime Rate-** The prime rate is the interest rate commercial banks charge their most creditworthy customers, which are usually corporations.
- **Put-Call Ratio-** technical indicator demonstrating investors' sentiment. The ratio represents a proportion between all the put options and all the call options purchased on any given day.
- **Put Options-** An option contract giving the owner the right, but not the obligation, to sell a specified amount of an underlying security at a specified price within a specified time. This is the opposite of a call option,
- **Retail Investor-** Individual investors who buy and sell securities for their personal account, and not for another company or organization
- **Reverse Split-**the opposite of a conventional (forward) stock split, which increases the number of shares outstanding
- **Shareholder-**Shareholders are a company's owners
- **Short Covering-**refers to the purchase of the exact same security that was initially sold short, since the short-sale process involved borrowing the security and selling it in the market.

- **Short Interest**-Short interest can be expressed as a percentage by dividing the number of shares sold short by the total number of outstanding shares
- **Shorting**-Initially you borrow certain stocks, sell them and later, if possible, when the price drops, you buy it in the open market to replace the borrowed stocks.
- **Short Interest Ratio**-the number of shares shorted divided by the number of shares available for trading
- **Short Squeeze**-A situation in which a heavily shorted stock or commodity moves sharply higher, forcing more short sellers to close out their short positions and adding to the upward pressure on the stock.
- **Stock Dividend**-A dividend is a distribution of a portion of a company's earnings, decided by the board of directors, to a class of its shareholders.
- **Stock Exchange Market**-Organized and regulated financial market where securities (bonds, notes, shares) are bought and sold
- **Stock Option**-A right to buy or sell specific securities or commodities at a stated price within a specified time.
- **Stock (or Ticker) Symbol**-string of letters used to identify a stock, bond, mutual fund, ETF or other security traded on an exchange
- **Stop Limit Order**-A stop order that designates a price limit.
- **Subprime**-borrowers with a tarnished or limited credit history.
- **Venture Capital**-Money provided by investors to startup firms and small businesses with perceived long-term growth potential. This is a very important source of funding for startups that do not have access to capital markets.

- **VIX Index**- trademarked ticker symbol for the CBOE Volatility Index, a popular measure of the implied volatility of S&P 500 index options; the VIX is calculated by the Chicago Board Options Exchange (CBOE).

5 DISCLAIMER

DISCLAIMER & NOTIFICATIONS

The author shall not be liable for any losses incurred during trading or any related activities; or any other damage. This book is written solely for educational purposes. We may or may not buy or sell securities mentioned. Sources of information are believed to be reliable, but they are in no way guaranteed to be complete or without error; and there is no guarantee of accuracy. Recommendations, opinions or suggestions are given with the understanding that subscribers acting on information assume all risks involved. It is each subscriber's responsibility to decide which, if any opinion, and in what manner to use this information. Past performance is no guarantee of future results. Hypothetical or simulated performance results have certain inherent limitations; and they do not represent actual trading. A purchase or gift can NOT also include personal discussions on an individual basis via phone or email or in person. <u>Once again, a subscription or purchase or gift can NOT also include personal discussions on an individual basis via phone or email or in person.</u>

Editor: Lalana Fernando   Email: Prosperitystocks@yahoo.com

www.ingramcontent.com/pod-product-compliance
Lightning Source LLC
Chambersburg PA
CBHW070402190526
45169CB00003B/1080